2

# Fred Taylor
# Yorkshire Cheesemaker

37200

# Fred Taylor
## Yorkshire Cheesemaker

*by* **W.R.Mitchell**

**CASTLEBERG**
2000

*In this series:*
TOT LORD AND THE BONE CAVES
EDITH CARR: LIFE ON MALHAM MOOR
EDWARD ELGAR IN THE YORKSHIRE DALES

A **Castleberg** Book.

First published in the United Kingdom in 2000.

Text © W R Mitchell 2000.

The moral right of the author has been asserted.

ISBN 1 871064 54 6

Typeset in New Baskerville, printed and bound in the United Kingdom by Lamberts Print & Design, Station Road, Settle, North Yorkshire, BD24 9AA.

Published by Castleberg, 18 Yealand Avenue, Giggleswick, Settle, North Yorkshire, BD24 0AY.

# Contents

| | |
|---|---|
| Introduction | 7 |
| Life with Grannie | 9 |
| Plenty of Pig Meat | 15 |
| Milking Time | 18 |
| Off to Work | 20 |
| To the Dairy | 33 |
| Working for the Dinsdales | 37 |
| In Production | 39 |
| At Fairfield Mill | 41 |
| A Dairy at West Marton | 43 |
| Reflections | 45 |

## The Illustrations

Cover photographs by WR Mitchell

Title page drawing by Brian Waters

Sketches of Dalesfolk by Ernest Forbes, who toured the region in the 1930s

Sketch of Daleswoman by Fred Lawson

Curlew sketch by Richard Clapham

Lapwing portrayed by E Jeffrey

## A Yorkshire Dales
## Auction Mart

Fred Taylor grew up at a time when a Dales farmer's
favourite cow was a shorthorn

## Introduction

# Oh, Swaledale's good for horses
# And Wensleydale for cheese...

**P**rofessor Moorman singled out Wensleydale for cheese – and rightly so – yet it was produced in other dales, including Dentdale, where Fred Taylor, the subject of this book, was born and reared.

The first Dales cheese was made from sheep's milk. Kit Calvert, of Hawes, credited the monks of Jervaulx Abbey with introducing into the Yorkshire Dales the type of cheese that has the generic name of "Wensleydale." Cheese, in its various forms, has been known for at least four thousand years. I can imagine the Norse folk, who in summer took their cattle and sheep to the high fells, locked up the nutrition and flavour of milk for later consumption by making cheese.

Wensleydale cheese, as we know it today, is associated with a creamery at Hawes which prides itself on its local connection and uses milk produced in the upper dale. This type of cheese is produced in dairies elsewhere. In the pre-factory days, the cheese was made at farms over a wide area of the dale-country.

The marketing board describes Wensleydale as "a creamy white cheese, made from a finely cut curd that is lightly pressed, leaving it with a high moisture content that makes this cheese slightly crumbly and flaky. Ripened for only up to three weeks, it should be eaten while young and fresh to appreciate its gentle honeyed after-taste."

Fred Taylor points out that a good cheese depends basically on the state of the soil and the "herb of the land." Years ago, before widespread ploughing and re-seeding with a ryegrass mix to give an early, lush growth of grass for an increasing dairy herd, a connoisseur could have told the difference between a cheese made on one side of the river of its native dale and a cheese made at a farm on the other side.

A cheese-maker of old considered that the best product was in "fog-time," fog being the second growth of grass. When Fred was working at Sedbergh, a cheese-buyer used to say: "I'll tak every cheese that has a fur coat on it." So they selected for him cheese with mould about an inch long. "That man knew it would be a lively cheese."

Today, over wide areas, though not entirely in the upper dale country, where grants are available to retain typical old hay meadows, the mown grass is ensiled. Cheese-making has been speeded up from a time when about four and a-half hours elapsed between introducing "starter" and salt.

Wensleydale is a "new" cheese. It is up to the individual whether he or she likes it young or not-so-young. It has tended to be more acidic because of the impervious packing and the necessity to get the moisture out. To Fred, the best Wensleydale is one that has been made moist, cloth-bound – and turned over on its shelf every day for a week.

He was a farmer's boy who, when he left school, was bound to a local farmer for a specified term for next to nothing and with no limited except time itself to the number of hours to be worked. A shilling changed hands and there was a handclasp to seal the bargain. "I was more or less fast. If I had left the farm before my time, no one else in the district would have employed me." When Fred Taylor began cheese-making, he was dealing with 50 gallons of milk at a time. Mostly it was milk from Shorthorn cattle, though in the Sedbergh area one chap had Ayrshires, which were said to produce the ideal milk for cheese-making.

In t'auld days, cheese-makers were adaptable. If a farmer said: "Fred – mek us a cheese for haytime," he turned out one that weighed 10 pounds and the cost was met by "knocking off 10 gallons from the next lot of milk to be delivered. You could reckon that each pound of cheese represented one gallon of milk." Now the Friesian cow is supreme and the through-put at a dairy is colossal compared with the days when Fred's cheese-making career began.

Though retired, his opinions are sought by creameries in many parts of the land. He has been saddened by national events of recent times that have led to the decline of the Yorkshire Dales dairy industry and, overall, to the impoverishment of many of Fred's old friends, the Dales farmers.

# One
## *Life with Grannie*

**B**orn in 1927, Fred grew up in the austere 1930s. He was reared at Butterpots, a "normal-sized mixed farm" on the snug side of Deepdale and with a splendid view of Whernside, the highest of the Three Peaks. The farm name was derived from limestone that was worn by the weather – by rain and frost – into the shape of the old crocks in which butter was kept.

Deepdale, a tributary of Dentdale, has a string of little hill farms, approached from a road that begins in the cobbled streets of Dent Town and, after traversing Deepdale and Kingsdale, arrives in the vicinity of Ingleton. The road, an old track, was tarmaced less than half a century ago.

"At Butterpots, we mew [mowed] about twenty acres and there were two allotments [fell grazings] went with it. They were enough for us to keep just over a hundred sheep." Fred's father, William, who was a native of Clapham, had been a hill farmer for many years and so he was able to cope with the conditions created by thin soils, cloudy summers and long, long winters. Anyone could farm when it was sunny. It was in winter, when the "snow dogs" were howling, and the days seemed little more than a blink between two long nights, that men were sorted out from the lads.

The Taylors were as "well off" as any other family in the dale, which means they were just managing to keep their heads above water. "I can remember hearing my mother and father talking. Dad said: 'There's not going to be much for the children this Christmas'." Like so many Dales holdings, Butterpots was almost self-sufficient. "We couldn't afford to buy anything," says Fred. Apart from a score of Shorthorn cows of various ages and a couple of Dales horses, small and versatile, the family had their own pigs, hens, some raspberry bushes and plum trees. They made butter but not cheese, though Butterpots had a cheese-press and, says Fred, every farm had what had served as a cheese-room, even if it was in a cart-house.

The sheep were Swardles [Swaledales]. As far back as Fred can remember, trade was indifferent. "The men who bought sheep knew if there was a lot of grass or it had been a poor growing season. If it was poor, they would get the sheep cheap in the autumn. The farmer couldn't keep them all at home." Fred remembers Dad going to market with his crop of lambs and coming back to say to Mother: "I've near given 'em away." They had their good times as well.

Butterpots and some other little farms in steep-sided Deepdale stood well over 1,000 ft above sea level, being open to the elements. Father ran sheep on Whernside, a tabular hill that formed a dramatic backdrop to the view. Butterpots was in sled-country, with many places where it was unwise to venture with a horse and cart because the cart would "throw ower." At haytime, only an idiot mowed down-bank. The steep ground meant that a horse would find it difficult to pull even the smallest machine upwards. "We scythed it down both sides of a meadow and then used the horse and cutter across the field."

Most sleds were unshod [had no metal runners] but ran as easy over the springy turf of the upland fields as on winter snow. Billy Middleton, the joiner at Dent, made the sleds that were intended to be horse-drawn. Apart from the basic model, there was a "trail-cart," known in the northern dales as a "coup" – a sort of tub on a sled used for taking t'muck out where you couldn't get with a horse-drawn cart. This type had iron runners.

A sled would run on any sort of surface if there was a good horse in front. "We used to go along the Occupation Road, gathering bracken for bedding down young stock. Anyone can make a sled straight. A true hay sledge is up at t'front and up at t'back. It's bent at both ends. It depended on what you wanted to pay. Billy would make you a big 'un or a little 'un. If you wanted a reight good 'un, he'd make it bevelled.

Jet, a favourite sled-pulling horse at Butterpots, began life with a black coat that gradually became white with increasing age. When Jet died, Fred's mother would not hear of it being taken to a knacker's yard. That horse had been like one of the family. "We had to take it to the high side of the farm and bury it."

The housework was marginally less exacting than haymaking. Fred recalls Butterpots Farm as a place where the ground floors were flagged, covered here and there by "coconut matting." T'kitchen was conspicuous by its austerity. Here was a big range, with a fireplace flanked by boiler and oven. They demanded a weekly application of black-lead. The furniture was plain but durable. Damp clothes and wash-leathers hung from a rack suspended from the ceiling; the rack could be raised or lowered.

In the parlour [sitting room] pegged rugs had been laid. "In winter, me and my brother Miles had to cut up old clothes into strips and pass them to Mum and Dad, who spent many an hour making rugs." The main passage had been flagged. Fred can remember when it was rough and when father decided to have it cemented. The illumination was provided by paraffin lamps and candles purchased from Batty's of Dent, who made a round of the dale weekly.

The capacious roof of Butterpots Farm sheltered Fred's grandparents – Christopher and his wife, whose Christian name Fred could never remember. "We always called her Grannie." She was tall, bony, clad mainly in black. "I can't remember her in anything except black, though her brat [apron] had blue stripes." They were thinner and closer together than you'd find on a butcher's apron.

Grannie, bless her, was one of the last of the old-time hand-knitters of Dent, following the custom of rocking in her chair and crooning as she knitted with four metal needles, one of them implanted in the head of a wooden knitting-stick, which looked like a dagger and was tucked behind a cloth belt that was attached to her pinafore. The traditional belt of Dentdale was made of leather. Fred treasures that old knitting stick, the highly polished wood of which is off-set by a brass ferrule. Grannie's steady progress while knitting was indicated by the tapping of one foot with the completion of every stitch. It was a conspicuous tap, for Grannie always wore clogs.

Grannie was always knitting socks, either for the three lads in the family or for paying customers elsewhere in the dale. Her experience came in handy in winter, when she did most of her knitting. Not much daylight filtered into the living room during the day and a paraffin lamp or candle provided little light in the long evenings. Fred recalls: "Mother and Grannie would trim the lights every night, saying – 'Well, we'll 'etta leet up'."

Fred went to school in clogs. "I had to walk a total of six miles a day." Dad used to call clogs by the old dale name of carkers [caulkers], from the metal strips nailed on to the wooden sole to protect it. Fred was forever kicking out to make sparks fly and that was the quickest way of knocking them off. Dad would say: "Here's an awpenny [halfpenny] for a bit o' Spanish at dinner-time. Then go and get Tom Fawcett to put your carkers on." If you lost a carker off, you were wearin' on to t'wood. Dad reasoned that if a nail or two were not put in, he would have to go to the expense of buying another pair of clogs.

Tom, who made clogs, did the job of fettlin' up any that had been damaged. He did it while the customer waited, in stockinged feet. "I think he liked kids going. He was an oldish chap who spent a lot of time on his own. He used to ask kids what they had been doing that day. Fred says: "With clogs, you're on wood. Your feet are kept dry and warm. You had to sit in school all day. If you had worn shoes, you'd have been wet through. The wet never got through to your foot. The wood absorbed it. And there was nothing like a good clog for turning snow-broth [the snow as it melted]."

Fred thought nothing of his daily walk to and from school at Dent. It was a walk that had begun when he was five years of age; he then had the company of his brother Miles. Traditionally Fred wore a beret, a big muffler, a coat and breeches that had been worn by Miles and handed down, as was the Dales custom. There were clogs on his feet. "We were as well off as any other family at that time." Fred cannot remember being late for school.

After being at lonely little Butterpot, a jaunt to Dent was exciting. Fred's clogs encountered cobbles and he saw with interest the great slab of Shap granite that had been reared to provide a memorial fountain. Everyone spoke of Adam Sedgwick, the man who was commemorated, with a respect edging up to awe. He had been the classic case of a local man who had made good. He had been to t'village school but became a professor of geology at Cambridge and was in Queen Victoria's circle of friends.

Fred had already had an introduction, through Grannie, to hand-knitting. Now he discovered it was once widely practised, using wool brought weekly by cart from Kendal. Everyone – men, women, children – knitted furiously. The income eked out that of the farm at a time when farming was going through a lean period.

As Fred grew up, "I wanted bits o' something for miself. I said to my mother: 'Can I have some pocket money?' She said: 'We'll have to ask thee father'. So I said to me dad: 'Can I have a bit o' pocket money?' He said: 'If thou wants pocket money, lad, thou'll have to go and addle [earn] it'. As mother said, with tears coming in her eyes: 'If we could, we would – but we have nowt'."

On his way home from school, Fred – aged eleven – passed a farm where there were a lot of wall-gaps. "I though to myself: 'I'll go to John Oversby and ask him if he wants his gaps putting up'. I was a good hand at walling'. I went to him and he said: 'Aye – tha can put me some gaps up'. I knew he had a lot round t'house and I thought he'd get me to do them.

"Instead, he said: 'Thou can start reight up on top o' Whernside'. He doubtless thought: 'That'll knock 'im out'. I said: 'Reight – when have I got to start?' He said: 'Tha can start now'. I had to walk right up to the top of Whernside at night to put those gaps up. I put 'em up. And he paid me. Then he said I could put gaps up round t'house."

When Fred had grown up and was collecting bygones connected with the Dales daily trade, he went to John Oversby and explained matters. "I said that when I was a lad, I'd done him a good turn. He remembered what had happened and said: 'I'll see what I can do'. He let me have quite a lot of things. John was a bit of a tight 'un and hadn't thrown much away.

Fred recalls that John let him have one thing at a time. He'd say: "Tha's not gettin' no more today. Tha hetta come again another time." He'd wanted Fred to go and see him. They could talk about similar interests. "He was usually a quiet chap. I think he was part relation to my mother. In the end, I got churns, his butter-bowl, prints and his cooling system."

# Two

## Plenty of Pig Meat

Fred has sharp memories of the "sittings." On a winter's night, local farmers went from one farm to another. It was known as "camping." One or two men, meeting in Dent Town, would chat awhile, then it was agreed to "go up to so-and-so's house and sit a bit." The old friends might talk about local things and what was going on in the dale. At one farm they might also play a game of dominoes. At another, the sport would be "table billiards." They were inclined to drink summat stronger than lemonade.

If anyone visited a farm at "back-end time," when almost every farmer had a pig or two, he'd be invited to "come and hev a look at mi pig." Then, says Fred, "there'd be half an' hour of talking about it." The day on which the pig was to meet its end was generally a "boon day." It was a combined effort by several families.

Folk got fed-up of pig-stuff in wintertime. "They all worked it so there was a pig-killing every week-end and, naturally, everybody was invited to take part. If mi dad was killing this week-end, Jimmy Bentham would be killing next week-end. Pigs had to be killed in the winter season because it was good 'keeping' weather."

The main pig-killer in the dale was known as t'butcher. When Fred was a schoolboy, he was Jack Akrigg, an easy-going chap who might "land up" at a farm half an hour late. "The farmer used to get agitated because he'd got big set-pan on. You needed lots of boiling water. It was used when you were scraping t'bristles off, which had to be done before the pig went cold."

When the pig was dead, it was hung up for a day so the flesh could set before the carcass was cut up. Some processes began immediately and there wasn't a thing wasted. Blood was "catched" for black puddings. The head was made into brawn. "My mother used to say to t'butcher – that was Roly Burton – I want a bit o' beef for t'pig head. That was all she said. He knew what she wanted. And he'd sell her a lump o' beef. While brawn was being made, there was a horrible smell. But when you put brawn on to your bread, it was beautiful."

Pig feet were boiled. When Fred went to work for Anthony Hargreaves at Rigg End, for six months, he returned to the farmhouse for his dinner one day to find a pig foot on his plate. "That's all there was – a pig foot and bread and butter. My mother had never served anything like that. I didn't know how to start of it. There was a bit of grisly meat on it. Anthony said: 'This looks good' and put some mustard on his plate. I followed suit and I did what he did. I can't say I enjoyed it."

One man who had the job of chopping the carcass at a Dales farm should have severed it down the middle of the back but he made such a hash of it that the farmer said: "Go easy – or thou'll have both lugs [ears] on one side." Fred recalls the "guessing," when each person tried to assess the pig's weight. "This meant that on t'neet after, they had an excuse to turn up for t'pig killing supper. Everyone wanted to known whose guess had been most accurate because everybody thought they were experts. The winner got sixpence."

To preserve the pork, a block of salt, weighing over 20 lb was bought, together with "a bit of salt petre for rubbing into the bones." The salted meat was put into a milk-lead. This was a deep metal tray once used for separating cream from the milk. It could be found on a ledge in the "buttery," a cold little room with a flagged floor.

The salted meat was carefully deposited in layers, with the hams at the bottom, overlaid by the shoulders and with the flitches [middle part of the pig] on top. It was all covered in a white cloth – the sort they used for making the bags you bought your flour in. Mother used to boil the bags until they were white.

Salting was quite an art. "My dad was a good salter. He'd rub the hams longer than t'others because they were to be kept in salt the longest." Dad was economical in his farming practice and put the pig-cheek into salt. "That was fetched out after about a week. It was hung up from one of the hooks on the kitchen ceiling. The flitches were the next to be lifted from the milk-lead, after about a fortnight. Then t'shoulders followed, three weeks after being put down."

The hams, which were always kept for the last, was kept in salt for a month. "A ham was boiled on a special occasion."

# Three
## *Milking Time*

In the merry month of May, there was jubilation when Grass Day arrived and the milk cattle were turned out of the shippons to graze the fields. Some Dales farmers were such sticklers to tradition they let out their cows on the traditional date, the 20th, even if they were being bombarded with hailstones. A farming couple awoke one May morning after a night during which it snowed hard, and saw that the cows were up to to their hocks in snow. The farmer said to his wife; "Ay, lass – we must have slept all summer."

The Taylors, like their neighbours, kept Shorthorn cattle. The milk remained on the farm, being used for human consumption or, with the cream separated, converted into butter, the blue [skimmed] milk being allocated to the young stock. Milking the cattle was then, as now a twice-daily ritual, with the added complication that stock was spread over a number of barns. Most of the animals were milked at an outbarn, the milk being transported to the farmhouse in a back-can, which was a small metal kit, with one side shaped to fit a man's back, complete with a harness.

When anyone was buying a back-can, the tinsmith would ask if he wanted an "uphill" or a "downhill" can. Cattle were dispersed over a number of outbarns, some situated higher and others lower than the farmhouse. Anyone transporting milk from the lower barns would have a five-gallon can, whereas those with high barns, who would be transporting milk downhill, could usually manage a can with a capacity of seven gallons.

The average Dales farmer kept sufficient cattle to provide milk for the use of the family and to make butter that might be sold or swapped for groceries. Fred recalls that one day a week was allocated for butter-making. The new milk was poured into "leads" to settle; then the blue [skimmed] milk was drained away, leaving the cream on the sloping sides.

This cream was stored in a crock until the weekly churning. Fred was expected to lend a hand in turning the heavy churn. A slapping sound indicated when the cream had become butter. Farmers worried little, if at all, about hygiene. One of them would say: "Milk tastes of nowt till t'cow's hed its foot in t'bucket."

No longer on a little Dales farm do you hear the swish of milk hitting the side of a pail. On the few remaining dairy farms, the milk is stored in refrigerated tanks. Fred tells of a man who had a milk-cooler – a sort of fluted apparatus down which the milk coursed, to have its temperature lowered by a flow of cold water within. A visiting inspector compliment-ed him on the way he was maintaining his cooler. It looked just like new, which it was. It had never been used.

The farmer had installed a milk-cooler, as he must, but carried on with the family tradition of putting the laden milk kits into a local trough to cool off. Water coming straight from the ground was much colder than the water that emerged from a tap.

# Four
## Off to Work!

Fred's first job on leaving school in 1941 was working for Anthony Hargreaves, of Rigg End. "He'd had a cow-house in Liverpool and was a real hard-working sort of chap." Fred did not want farm work because [and he laughs] "it was *hard* work." Yet as a lad who had just left school there was nothing else for him to do.

"Anthony used to come a-sitting, so Dad knew him well. Dad said to me: 'Well, Fred, you'll have to work. We can't keep you at home'." He went across to see Anthony and it was arranged that he would work for the old chap for six months, from November until April, his wage being £20. He put the "fixing" shilling into Fred's hand and he was "erl'd," which was a word he had not heard before. "What it meant was that if I had left my job and gone to somebody locally, I would not have been employed. There was no mention of 'time off' or anything like that. I had to work till t'jobs were done."

Fred's mother gave him his stuff in a tin box. There were some fustian breeches, clogs, an old shirt or two. "And off I went to Rigg End, a farm that stood reight on t'side o' Whernside. It was a cold place and I went there in a hard winter." Those were the days when winter meant snow which, if it came with a north-easterly wind, squeaked underfoot. A blizzard isolated the remote farmsteads and soon altered the familiar contours of the land.

Fred was blistered and frost-bitten as he strove to do the farm work. "I had the job of watering the young stock at the outbarns. I had to go and break t'ice every morning. When I went home, my mother used to say: 'How are you going on?' I'd say: 'Grand'. I hated it."

Fred, beginning work at Rigg End, was at a farm similar in basics to that of his father but more intensive. "You were always at it, carrying hay from place to place or using a back-can. I was only 14 years old when I was carrying seven gallons on my back and a laden bucket in either hand. I was a big lad, but that didn't make any difference. Size didn't count. A farm man was expected to do it. Meanwhile, Anthony was carrying a bucket holding a few eggs."

It was what Fred now terms "a breaking in." He started work at 6 a.m. on a normal day, working through till 6 p.m. "At lambing time, I worked till six, then went out with the farmer till bedtime." None of the milk produced at the farm left the place as milk. "We made nearly all our milk into butter. First of all, the milk was set into basins and in due course the cream was skimmed off using part of a cow horn which had been shaped to suit the job."

The cream was kept in a special pot for the week, and "went off" to the stage at which it was churnable. "You put one lot of cream on top of another and if you want to be – as we are now – bacteria-minded, the lactic acid of the milk was growing all the time and made it easier to break into butter."

Thursday was butter-making day. "The lad's job was to turn the churn." Fred turned the churn for Anthony's wife, who was the butter-maker of the family. The residue, which was known as "blue milk" was used for calf-feed, though some of the butter-milk was taken to the kitchen, to be made into scones. The butter was patted into "pounds" using Scotch Hands [small wooden bats with fluted surfaces].

Anthony's wife then reached for a butter-print, which was made of sycamore, a wood that did not taint the milk. She marked each pound with a distinctive trade-mark. The Taylor family used the emblem of a swan. A trio of thistles marked the butter produced at the farm of Jackie Bentham. Poor butter might be a consequence of the poor state of the land. Anyone buying butter at the shop looked for an emblem they could trust.

Bad butter might be a consequence of working with utensils that were not clean. They acquired a foreign bacteria, which mean it was off-flavoured. If not enough butter-milk had been taken out after churning, moisture was left in the butter. Anyone who bought cheap butter was buying a lot of water and the possibility of a poor flavour.

"We carried butter down to Batty's shop at Dent in two big baskets. If folk at Dent Town complained the weather was cold, I used to say: 'You want to get up to Rigg End, where it's blowing off Whernside'. At snow-time, it filled all t'dykes every night."

Work extended over six and three-quarter days a week. "There wasn't talk of time-off. You set to work when work was there." Anthony kept a few Shorthorn cattle, "little hardy beggers – but quiet and placid." During the time Fred was at Rigg Farm, they never lost a cow. Anthony, having been in a milk-house at Liverpool, like many another raised in the little western dales, was well schooled on keeping stock healthy.

Anthony could sometimes be persuaded to talk about those cow-houses. Animals were kept in an urban setting, often at the end of a terrace of houses, where special accommodation had been built. Every scrap of fodder had to be imported – and the muck as well as the milk was exported. The dream of most cow-keepers was to return to the native dale – to Garsdale or Dentdale – with enough money to buy a small holding.

Occasionally, when Anthony had to doctor one of the cows at Rigg End, he put the medicine into an old cow horn and tipped the stuff directly into the cow's mouth. Two bovine complaints were "wooden tongue" and "scour," the last-named resulting from feeding the animal some bad hay. The Dales name for bovine diarrhoea was "skitters." Anthony would say, dolefully: "It's getten t'skitters."

There were "concoctions of all sorts" and homely remedies included oatmeal. Fred knew a farmer who, when he had a cold, took one of the preparations intended for animals. "He thought if it was good for t'cows, it'll be good for me. It used to mend him up."

True Shorthorns had little curly horns. If a cow had horns that inclined upwards, Anthony would say: "There's a bit of Ayrshire in it." The farmer was "nobbut a lile [little] chap but he had speed and dexterity when milking by hand. He would sit on a three-legged stool, wearing his cap with the neb at the back so he could rest his head on the cow's flanks and work the teats for all he was worth.

He would then glance at Fred, who could not keep up with this master-milker, and say: "If you keep going, lad, t'froth'll bring all t'muck out." This was true. As Fred watched, the froth poured over the edge – along with bits of grass and other objects classifiable as muck.

When a group of heifers, coming up to calving, shot a lot o' teat [the teats were elongated, like candles] one animal was inclined to tread on the teat of another, causing damage that slowed up the milking process. One evening, Anthony, when milking an animal with too much teat, asked Fred to hold the tail, which he did, though it was seven o'clock and he wanted to go to the Reading Room in Dent to play billiards. Suddenly, the cow swished its tail, which slipped out of Fred's hand and hit the farmer "right at back o' t'lug." Anthony shook his head sadly and remarked: "Thou'd better be going, lad; tha can't even 'od a cow tail."

Fred liked to play billiards with his friends. "One night, I was milking a cow and said: 'Can I go to Dent?' It was six o'clock then. He said: 'Oh well, tha can go if thou's nowt better to do'. I said: 'Do you want me to stop?' He said he'd like me to stop while it was lambing time. And there was I – fast till bedtime. He had quite a lot of sheep that were lambing. It wasn't hard work at that time of day."

Fred learnt a lot from Anthony simply by standing and watching him. "He'd smoke his pipe and say: 'She'll lamb afore morning'. I'd got interested and used to wonder how he knew. I'd see him walk about, studying his sheep. He used to get up during t'night and wander about with a lantern. He virtually lived with his sheep."

When his time was up, he had worked a seven-day week, "with just four hours off." Says Fred: "I'll not say I enjoyed it – but everybody did it." Mum said: "You must have done well for him; he's given you £6 more." Fred replied that he had invariably worked till bedtime, especially in lambing time. The farmer was getting old and needed someone to catch the lambs.

His chief memories were of winter – a terrible winter, with the ground plated with snow and ice. Fred was determined to move "lower down the dale." Though Fred was never formally hired after his experience at Rigg End, he was fond of attending the hirings at New Road, Kendal, and seeing how others were faring. He will never forget the sight of farmers basing their opinion of a labourer purely on the strength of his muscles. They felt the upper arm and asked those who passed the test if they could milk a cow. That was enough to secure them employment. "At the end of the day, poor lads who were able but weakly ended up jobless."

Fred with some milk churns [kits]. Watering milk was not unusual. One dale farmer said he never begrudged paying the water rate. Another hammered one side of the churn so the milk level would be fractionally higher.

*Above:* Dent Town, showing the Adam Sedgwick memorial fountain.

*Left:* Sedbergh. Cheese production took place at Farfield.

Two photographs at Farfield, Sedbergh.
*Above:* Farfield staff, photographed when operations were about to be trans-
ferred to West Marton.
*Below:* Inside the mill, where all the operations were performed by hand.

**FRED TAYLOR SQUEEZES OUT THE WHEY FROM A SAMPLE OF CHEESE TO BE TESTED FOR LACTIC ACID.**

*Above:* One of the lorries that transported milk from the farms to the dairy at West Marton, 1959. *Below:* Noel Stockdale, the highly-regarded chairman of the company, in the West Marton cheese store, and Fred, with metal cheese press.

PART OF THE DAIRY AND CHEESE-MAKING MUSEUM AT WEST MARTON.

A DEEPDALE FARMER
OF MORE RECENT TIMES

# Five
## To the Dairy

When the Dinsdales began the factory production of Wensleydale cheese at Dent in 1926, cheese-making had been a farmhouse occupation that had, for some years, taken second place to the production of butter. Says Fred: "It was similar to butter-making. There was a 'kettle' which stood beside the fire and into which the night's milk was poured to keep warm, stimulating the development of lactic acid. The milk from the morning milking, which was still warm, was poured into the kettle and rennet added as a coagulant."

It might take one or even two hours to "set," depending on the amount of lactic acid. "Mind you," says Fred, "they did not know what lactic acid was in those days. They just allowed it to set. You more or less went by smell or feel – that's what I did when I started working at the cheese factory for Frank Dinsdale."

In the old farmhouse method, it was cut into pieces using a knife. It was then suspended in a cloth to let the whey drain out. What remained was the curd. This was broken up, salt added and the cheese was put into a mould and pressed. "If your cheese kept a long time, you had obviously had a good cheese. If it didn't, then something was wrong."

The involvement of the Dinsdales in local cheese production dated from the arrival at Dent of a young man called James Dinsdale, a native of Wensleydale. He carried on a grocery business, Messrs J Dinsdale and Sons, that depended largely on barter. With little money in the dale, he exchanged groceries and cattle-cake for farmhouse products like butter, eggs and cheese. Living with the Dinsdales was an aunt, also a native of Wensleydale, who was a first-rate maker of farmhouse cheese.

It was largely at her instigation that the Dinsdales went into cheese-making in a big way.

Frank Dinsdale, one of the three sons of the founder of the firm, and the man who made the Dent creamery thrive, was a small, stoutish, reflective man. He had the support of Mabel, his wife, who was equally busy. Frank had toured Dentdale and Deepdale collecting surplus butter and eggs from the farms. Frank's man, with horse and cart, followed round with a butter-box and egg-crate picking up the produce and, on the following day, returning to the farms with maize, bran and a popular dog food.

Says Fred, who has clear memories of that period: "It was a barter. So much butter, so much linseed cake. So many eggs, so much food for t'dog. Not much money changed hands." Frank carted what he had acquired up the winding hill to Dent station, where it was consigned by rail to the market in Leeds.

In the 1920s, Frank opened a small dairy with the object of making cheese from surplus milk. His scheme was welcomed, for these were the Hungry Thirties, when butter had been made for eightpence or ninepence a pound and milk sold for sixpence a gallon. The Dinsdales paid sevenpence a gallon.

The extra penny made all the difference to a local farmer. You might say, therefore, that the Dinsdales were the salvation of dalesfolk. Fred remembers his mother talking enthusiastically about the dairy and its demand for milk, saying: "This is grand!"

When the Dinsdales first had their eyes on the surplus milk in Deepdale and Cowgill, which lay updale from Dent Town, they contacted Jack Middleton, who lived at the head of Deepdale. Jack was the proud owner of a strong dappled horse called Blossom and a good-sized milk-float. When he agreed to collect milk on a daily basis, he was supplied with three 17 gallon churns [kits]. Each farmer was provided with a gallon measure.

Within Fred's recollection, Jack's son, Gordon, did the morning milk round, starting at the top of the valley, stopping at each farm, where he was greeted by the farmer carrying buckets of new milk. This was measured and poured into one of the big kits for transfer to Dent. Fred never knew what business arrangement was reached, but in days when "not a lot of money as such changed hands," it is likely that Frank let Jack

Middleton have "a bit o' shopping." The main consideration was that local farmers had a new source of income in straitened times.

Fred remembers the milk-float well, for at the age of five he began a regular round trip, six miles in all, from Butterpots Farm to school. Sometimes he "cadged" a lift on Gordon Middleton's horse-drawn outfit. Gordon had taken pity on the lile lad wearing a cut-down coat, fustian breeches, muffler and beret who clomped along wearing clogs. If truth be known, coat and breeches had been passed down in the family when his elder brother grew out of them.

The most exciting journey was when Blossom and the milk-float and Tidy Middleton, the postman, who drove "an old Austin 7 soapbox thing," met at a corner. "We went up bank, tipped up, and milk went everywhere. Gordon said: 'I think it's a bit dangerous; you'd appen not come again'. I didn't cadge a lift for a day or two, then soon got back into the old routine."

From relying on a farmer's milk-float, the Dinsdales acquired a small van, which enabled them to extend his commercial venture into Garsdale. He eventually got a small wagon. Nothing larger could be used on the narrow roads and even narrower bridges.

Though the firm strove to process clean milk, the processes were not as sensitive to hygiene as is the case today. Fred recalls that untreated milk was filtered through a cloth on its way into the hand-operated system. A man who was stirring with his hands would suddenly break off and go out to shovel coal on to the furnace; then, without washing his hands, would be "back into t'vat." And yet the cheese tasted good.

Frank sometimes recalled the hard inter-war years when a good deal of cheese was sold in Stockton, a place of heavy industry where workers developed good appetites. Except when there was a miner's strike and the pulse of local life beat slowly.

Said Frank: "I went up into the North-East to sell cheese. It was green [new] cheese. There was a coal strike. I met the miners' wives coming out of Stockton, with their prams and their babies. They were scratching in fields for taties and turnips. And I was trying to sell cheese to them."

That was when a salesman might demonstrate his ability, but Frank brought the cheese back home, unsold. "It nearly broke my heart seeing those women scrattin' in the fields," he told Fred.

A suspicion was entertained that some of the farmers who supplied the Dinsdales were "wattering" it to add to the bulk. One farmer said, with the hint of a smile, that he never begrudged paying t'water rate. Another, when visited by inspectors who were intent on testing the quality of his milk, was on his round with a horse-drawn float. He quickly stuck a sharp object into one of the horse's legs. The horse leapt forward, knocked over the kit and sent the (diluted) milk coursing towards the nearest drain.

# Six
## *Working for the Dinsdales*

For 21 years, Fred was employed by Frank Dinsdale at his farm which, known as Millbeck, lay just below Dent Town. This was where the cheese factory had been established. Fred, aged 14, had earned £20 for his half year at Rigg End. Now, in a more temperate setting and with thirty shillings a week, Fred was content.

Millbeck was a fairly large farm by Dentdale standards. "We mew about forty acres." Frank had installed Bob and Emily Johnson to look after the farm and Fred lodged with them. "It was like a home from home." Frank Dinsdale proved to be a man before his time. "Even today I can think of things he forecast that have come true. He supplied electricity to Dent and said to Fred the day would come when people would have no say who supplied electricity. It would all belong to one group and the customer would have to pay what the group demanded. There would be no competition..." That was years ago, before the word "nationalisation" had entered everyday speech.

Frank had a new shippon built and introduced a grass-drier. He put a six-inch pipe down the side of the beck flowing through his farm and had a dam on the allotment on the fell. Then, using a water-turbine, he generated electricity, which was also available to householders in Dent Town. When the supply became inadequate, he supplemented it using a diesel engine. He had one of the first tractors to be seen in the dale. "Frank was a bit better off than most and he liked to experiment."

Memories of the farm include "boon days," when neighbouring farmers worked together at such jobs as sheep-clipping. "They used to have a wash-place for sheep in t'river Dee. They'd run the sheep through. It got rid of dirt in the wool. We never washed ours."

For one boon-clip, Fred went on to the Crag with Bob, the chap he was staying with. "We were supposed to be rounding up sheep but mist came down and we were sitting on through-stones at the back of a wall for two or three hours waiting for it to lift. We found out afterwards it was sunny at Dent. We got back when it was nearly dinner-time. We should have been down by nine o'clock. Men were waiting to start clipping."

Sheep-clipping was hectic. "Lads used to catch sheep and bring them to the men who had a stock [clipping bench] apiece and clipped the sheep. Then lads had to mark 'em and roll up the wool. "You had to do it in a day. If you fetched your own sheep from the top, you couldn't hold them while you clipped 'em by yourself; so all the men went from farm to farm. Anyway, boon day was a grand day. Everybody had a good laugh and old-fashioned jokes were flying around.

Women went round with drinks in a big can. There was always tea available. The womenfolk also prepared food – tatie'ash [meat and potato pie]. Ham sandwiches and cakes – for the big feed that followed. It was, says Fred, "a nice way o' living."

# Seven

## *In Production*

The small dairy, in old farm buildings converted to the new use, stood behind Dinsdale's shop, opposite Dent Church. With six or seven employees, the cheese production at Dent was not to outgrow its status as a small family business. All the processes were undertaken by hand.

The Dinsdale family began with a vat of 50 gallon capacity. It was a jacketed vat, allowing for a flow of heated water around it. The capacity was extending to over 200 gallons and in 1950 the family moved their enterprise to Farfield Mill at Sedbergh. Here about 3,000 pounds of cheese were produced daily.

Fred, who was farm man at Millbeck, occasionally helped in the Dent Creamery. "I got to like it, so Frank Dinsdale took me on as such." Cheese could be made only at flush periods for milk, which meant for about a quarter of the year. Fog-time, using the Dales term for the second flush of grass in the meadows, was the busiest period for making cheese. It was mostly produced in September and October. When there was a lull in the supply of milk, the equipment was stripped down, overhauled and the premises were painted, for Frank kept his little team in employment the year through.

In days before milk was pasteurised, it was delivered to Dent in kits, by horse and cart, by motor van, car-hauled trailer or tractor and trailer. "The milk we accepted was either cooled or uncooled, clean or containing hayseeds and all manner of foreign bodies, as you might expect from farms where milking took place in what were basically dirty shippons and was handled without too much regard for hygiene."

Frank accepted such milk because he needed it if he was to keep the creamery profitable. "If he had refused milk, he would have also lost a valued customer for cow-cake. That chap was coming to his shop for goods." The milk was poured through a cloth that acted as a sieve and then ran into a bath where it was made up. The implements used during the cheese-making process, in addition to the human hand, was a piece of wood and a knife.

Making farmhouse cheese had taken about ten hours. At the creamery, cheese-making was vastly increased in scale and had the additional benefit of a meter that recorded acidity and was a control on quality. The creamery also had effective cooling facilities. Cheese could be produced in about six hours. At the peak of production, the dairy van was collecting from 112 farms and in one month 93,000 gallons were collected. All of it was made into cheese.

The Dinsdales were leaders in a number of local enterprises. "Frank had a tractor when a lot of people had horses or ponies. He built a new shippon when many folk were making do with the old type. He would annually have a tree felled and left to dry out, arranging for it to be taken to Old Dewdrop at Rash Mill to be sawn up. Dewdrop's ancient engine had to be cranked up to start it. He spoke about the engine as though he was talking to his wife. He'd say: 'I don't know what she'll be like this morning. She's bin a bit awk'ard'. None the less, he'd get the machine working."

The joiner, who was so named because of a leaky nose, was never in a hurry. Asked on a subsequent visit if the tree had been sawn, he'd say: "Nay – ah've bin busy." Frank would shuffle about, then put his hand into his back pocket and pull out one or two banknotes. Dewdrop would say: "Ah'll see if she'll start this morning." She invariably did. The fickle machine flapped and banged. Says Fred: "How she kept going I don't know... she did t'job all right."

# Eight

## *At Farfield Mill*

When in 1950 cheese production was switched to Farfield Mill at Sedbergh, Fred moved with the enterprise. The mill stood well clear of the town and had a backdrop in the Howgill Fells, big, rounded, grassy fells which, having no drystone walls, had their own special shadow pattern. The sheep of the Howgills were Rough Fells. The cattle were mainly Shorthorns, but the black-and-white Friesian, with its larger production of milk, was in the offing.

At Farfield, larger vats were installed. More farmers were turning to dairy stock and milk production was rising steeply. "When we got an acidity meter, Frank didn't like it. He said: 'The sooner you throw that away, the sooner you'll make proper cheese'. In a way he was right." Production peaked at 3,000 gallons a day.

Frank's inventiveness was to be seen on every hand, such as in the multi-use of water, which was piped back into a tank and used to wash down the floor at night. When Frank's wife became ill, he said to Fred: "I can't come down as much as I used to do. I shall have to sell it – or you'll have to take over." Fred was invited to become manager. He was twenty-one years of age. Now he had no stipulated hours. He worked as required – and got a bonus at the year end.

He insisted that everyone, "even the lad who cleaned the vats," should have a bonus for all contributed to the success of the cheese. If there was to be a special reward for Fred, it should be an addition to his wage.

The Farfield years were happy. He had taken over a creamery that in its heyday had business links with customers at home and overseas. One pre-Christmas season, cheese was despatched to thirty-one different countries. An engineering firm in Vancouver who sent for a hundred cheeses wrote again, after two years, to report that they were still enjoying them. Cheese was supplied to Royalty. The London trade also included orders from Harrods and Fortnum & Masons. Cheeses sent to Liverpool were intended for the Cunard liners.

The workers were farm-type people, drawn from the locality. "I was the manager, but there was no 'clocking-in'. We worked well together. It was a happy place. When a girl left to get married, a vat was partly filled with water and she was douked [dipped] in a little ceremony that caused much amusement."

When the firm of J Dinsdale & Sons closed down at Sedbergh, having been acquired by Associated Dairies of Leeds, the work was switched to West Marton and Fred, who was then living in Sedbergh, went with it. Here he was to have another twenty years of active service producing high quality cheese.

"We had a cat at Farfield Mill. It was called Smoky. All the staff loved here and she knew them well. Edmund Harper, who lived across the way from Farfield, said he would look after Smoky and see that she was fed. He was as good as his word, but the cat pined to death. Edmund went to the mill one day – and found her lying there, dead."

## Nine

# A Dairy at West Marton

Frank Dinsdale, who considered that Fred was "a good chap," had not paid for overtime. Instead, he provided his manager with a modest-sized car of his own choice. He bought a Mini-Cooper for £400. The car came in handy when Fred was commuting between Sedbergh and West Marton.

Fred now exchanged Sedbergh, with its dramatic background of rounded fells, for West Craven, where the hills were more like glorified hummocks, known as drumlins and left there on the melting of the glacial ice many thousands of years before. The dairy had been set up by the Nelson family, owners of Gledstone estate, for the benefit of local farmers. Milk was collected, bottled and transported to city customers.

Fred's mission was to set up a cheese-making operation, which he did, with an initial 7,000 gallons of milk a day. The figure crept up steadily to 35,000 gallons. When Associated Dairies decided to spend millions of pounds on updating their Marton Dairy, and introduced cheese-making here, Fred asked Noel Stockdale, a man with a background of dairying in the Dales who now presided over the big firm, if space could be left for a museum in which to display equipment connected with dairying, and especially the making of cheese.

This was arranged and there came into being a collection of over 150 times – what must surely be the most comprehensive record of the Dales dairy industry from the turn of the century to the coming of the Milk Marketing Board in 1933. The exhibits range in size from cardboard bottle caps to a hand-turned cream separator, from measures and ladles to a 6 cwt stone cheese press. A model was decked with items of clothing a typical milkmaid would have been wearing almost a century ago. "Every item of clothing, from the sleeve bibs to the bonnet, is genuine."

Some Dales farmers approached by Fred were reluctant to part with an item that he needed to fill a gap in the collection. "It took me ten years to persuade a farmer to sell me a unique cream separator that was still in perfect working order." Cheese vats and butter churns were other items that told the story of a once-thriving domestic industry that became centred in creameries.

"Some of the items were in a shocking condition when I found them. They had been thrown into barns and even on to scrap heaps, but with a lot of elbow grease, and with sand-blasting in the case of old milk churns, they have survived."

# Ten
## *Reflections*

What has changed over the years? Fred, who retired in January 2000 but still serves West Marton and the cheese-making industry in general as a grader, observes that the cow that produced the milk from which Wensleydale cheese was made was the Shorthorn, whereas today most of the cattle are Friesian. "I was taught that the Ayrshire cow's milk was ideal for cheese because of its small fat globules, but I'm sure the everyday housewife, shopping in a supermarket, is not interested in the size of fat globules or if the body is firm or weak. She does not concern herself with whether the texture is too open or too tight."

The grass has lost some of its naturalness through a greater use of fertiliser, mainly nitrogen and phosphates, also pesticides. "I sympathise with today's farmer because previously he had to use more fertilisers to increase production and be profitable and now he has to cut back because of over-production. Fifty years ago, a cow giving four gallons of milk a day was good. Now it has to produce almost double that amount to be profitable."

Winter feed is now mainly silage, as opposed to hay. "I'm sure that lots of people, including myself, miss the smell of newly mown and dried hay." At the creamery, the laboratory staff test for quality, fats and solids, antibiotics, salt and moisture levels – and more. "Years ago, when milk was received in churns [kits] we had a sniffer. He was a man with a good nose and his job was to detect sour milk. At one dairy, the sniffer rarely had a cigarette out of his mouth."

Fred observes that the cheese-maker of today has a reliable starter [a

45

milk souring culture] and an acidity meter. The appliances are made of stainless steel. With  mechanical stirring and cutting of the curd, the job is much less stressful than it was. "We had none of these, but we still managed to produce cheese that we thought was the best. My tutor used to say: 'Try and make a better cheese tomorrow than you have made today and you'll be a cheese-maker one day'."

Times have indeed changed. Gone is the hand-milking routine and the consignment of milk by horse and trap to the nearest railway station, from which it would be taken to the city. Gone is the blue lorry of the Milk Marketing Board with its load of milk kits. It represented an organisation which, set up in 1933, was through its monthly milk cheques to be a cornerstone in the Dales farming system.

Milking herds have virtually gone from the upper dales. In their place are suckler cows, being reared for beef. Fred is left with his memories. Wistfully, he recalls his days as a footballer. He was good enough to have a trial with Preston North End when the star was Tom Finney. He recalls the many characters of Dentdale, including Tidy, the postman, who had a crate at the back of his car into which he placed old hens he bought from the farming folk.

Cheese-making has provided Fred with a fascinating occupation as well as a livelihood. He has judged at many shows, including Nantwich, the largest, and he has given instruction about the making of English cheeses in Ireland and Denmark. With regard to the stronger English cheeses, he has a particular fondness for Double Gloucester. His sense of taste is such that he can identify where specific cheeses were made, this being possible because of the differences of land on which the cattle grazed.

When Fred talks about cheese-making to senior citizens, he is invariably asked: "Why doesn't cheese taste like it used to do?" He replies: "The short answer is that the cow hasn't had its foot in the bucket. And the sweat from the cheese-maker's nose-end no longer drops into the curd."

# Castleberg Books
*by the same author*

| | |
|---|---|
| Birds of the Lake District | £6.50 |
| Birds of the Yorkshire Dales | £6.50 |
| Ghost-hunting in the Yorkshire Dales | £5.99 |
| Music of the Yorkshire Dales | £5.99 |
| | |
| Sacred Places of the Lake District | £6.50 |
| Beatrix Potter – Her Life in the Lake District | £6.20 |
| The Lost Village of Mardale | £5.60 |
| | |
| Garsdale – History of a Junction Station | £6.50 |
| Mile by Mile on the Settle to Carlisle | £5.99 |
| The Men Who Made the Settle to Carlisle | £5.99 |
| | |
| Cuckoo Town (Memories of Austwick) | £6.50 |
| Life in the Lancashire Milltowns | £5.99 |
| | |
| Nowt's Same | £6.50 |
| You're Only Old Once | £4.99 |

*Mini biographies:*

| | |
|---|---|
| Tot Lord and the Bone Caves | £4.50 |
| Edith Carr – Life on Malham Moor | £4.50 |
| Edward Elgar in the Yorkshire Dales | £4.99 |

All **Castleberg** titles are available at good bookshops
or, in case of difficulty, please write to:

North Yorkshire Marketing,
22 Azerley Grove, Harrogate,
North Yorkshire HG3 2SY

We will be pleased to send you a complete list of titles
and an order form

No postage is charged on **Castleberg** books